Science in a Bottle

Science in a Bottle

by Sandra Markle
Illustrated by June Otani

SCHOLASTIC INC.

New York Toronto London Auckland Sydney

ISBN 0-590-47595-9

12 11 10 9 8 7 6 5 4 3 2   5 6 7 8 9/9 0/0

Printed in the U.S.A.   40

First Scholastic printing, April 1995

Contents

Before You Start

Can you pick up a bottle without touching it?
Can you make a fountain in a bottle?
Can you prove that an empty bottle isn't empty?
Can you raise "sea monkeys" in a bottle?

Yes, you can do all this and more! All you need are some materials you will find at home or can buy cheaply at a grocery, gardening store, aquarium supply store, or hardware store. Then do the activities in this book.

You'll discover science can help you do some exciting things.

You'll be using plastic and glass bottles of different sizes in all of the activities.

You don't have to buy any bottles — just recycle. Collect used containers. Peel off the labels. Have an adult remove any plastic ring left by a twist-off cap. Then wash the bottles out and set them in a dish drainer in the sink — upside down with the caps off — to dry.

Any bottles that you don't cut up you can also wash and use again. That way you can enjoy investigating and help the earth, too.

Remember

- Make sure you have all the materials you need before you start.

- Be careful using scissors and other tools.

- Clean up the work area after you finish your project.

- Conserve water. After doing an experiment, transfer clean water to a pail or watering can. Use the water to water plants, wash the car, bathe the dog, etc.

- Have fun!

Some Things You'll Need

Can You Pick Up a Bottle Without Touching It?

Does this sound like a magic trick? With a little science, you can do it two different ways and amaze your friends.

You'll need:

A 16-ounce plastic soft drink bottle
A plastic straw
A balloon

First, bend the straw about a third of the way from one end. Keep the straw bent while you slide it through the neck of the bottle.

Once inside the bottle, the straw will straighten slightly. Pull it up slowly until the hook formed by the bend touches both sides of the bottle. Continue to pull slowly and you'll have just enough of a connection to the bottle to lift it.

Now use the balloon to lift the bottle. Does that seem impossible? But you can do it — by adding air!

Insert the round balloon inside the bottle. Stretch the neck of the balloon out through the bottle top and blow into it. As soon as the balloon swells enough to press against both sides of the bottle, pinch the neck shut. Then lift the bottle.

Easy!

It's a Gas

What gives a soft drink its fizz? The answer is bubbles of carbon dioxide gas. The carbon dioxide gas is added to the soft drink solution before it's bottled. But if you've ever taken a sip of a soft drink that has gone flat, you know that something happens to this gas after the bottle is opened. Does it escape into the air? Try this experiment to find out.

You'll need:

3 identical 16-ounce bottles of a soft drink
3 balloons with mouths big enough to fit
    the neck of the bottles
A large bowl
A drinking glass

Put one soft drink in the refrigerator and leave the other two at room temperature overnight.

The next day, take the cap off one of the room temperature bottles. As soon as you take the cap off, pour a little of the soft drink into a glass. See all the bubbles rising to the surface and bursting? That's carbon dioxide at work.

Now quickly slip a balloon over the neck of the bottle. Slide it down far enough to cover the screw top ridges. Wait fifteen minutes. The balloon will puff up as it traps the escaping carbon dioxide gas.

Now use the other two bottles of soft drink to try another experiment. This time you'll find out whether or not chilling the soft drink will help it keep its fizz longer.

First, get the room temperature bottle and set it in a bowl full of hot water. Then take the cold bottle out of the refrigerator. Quickly take the caps off both bottles, cover the tops with balloons, and return the cold bottle to the refrigerator.

Wait fifteen minutes.

To check which bottle lost the most carbon dioxide gas, look at the balloons. The bigger the balloon, the more carbon dioxide was trapped.

COLD BOTTLE   WARM BOTTLE

Put the chilled bottle back in the refrigerator and replace the hot water in the bowl. Wait another fifteen minutes, then compare the balloons one more time.

If you were taking bottles of a soft drink along on a picnic, do you think it would be worthwhile to try to keep opened bottles chilled?

What's Inside the Empty Bottle?

The bottle may look empty — but it's not. It's full of air, as you will see when you do this activity.

You'll need:

A 2-liter plastic soft drink bottle
A balloon with a neck big enough to
    fit over the bottle's mouth
A large saucepan
A mixing bowl

Put the bowl in the sink and fill it with hot water. Fill the saucepan half full of cold water and set it on the counter close to the sink.

Slip the neck of the balloon over the top of the bottle. Set the bottle in the bowl of hot water. Hold the balloon steady.

The balloon will puff up as the heat makes the air molecules inside the bottle move apart. The more the air expands and rises, the more the balloon will puff up.

Now, quickly move the bottle to the pan of cold water. What happens to the balloon? What do you think is happening to the air inside the bottle?

Test Your Lung Power

Did you ever wonder how much air moves in and out of your lungs when you breathe? Is it a lot or only a little? Does it depend on how deep a breath you take?

Here's an activity that will let you find out.

You'll need:

A clear plastic 16-ounce soft drink or water bottle

A 2-gallon pail

A long flexible straw (the kind used in many portable drink bottles)

A permanent marker

A towel

You may want to ask a friend to help you with this activity.

First fill the pail nearly full of water. Push the bottle under water to fill it completely full. Ask your friend to hold the bottle straight up, keeping the opening underwater.

Slip one end of the straw inside the bottle. Breathe in as you normally do, but breathe out by blowing through the straw. Your breath forces air into the bottle, and the air

will push out some of the water. That's why the water bubbles up around the bottle.

Lift the bottle out and dry one side. Mark the water level.

Dunk the bottle again and repeat the test. This time, though, take a *really* deep breath and force out all the air you can. Did you push out more water than the first time? A lot more or only a little more?

Human lungs can hold more than a gallon of air. The amount of air flowing in and out of your lungs is important. It's inside the lungs that your body takes in oxygen and gives off the waste gas carbon dioxide. Oxygen is carried by the blood throughout the body to the cells, the body's basic building blocks. There it is combined with food nutrients to produce the energy your body needs to grow and to be active.

Now, think about times when you breathe faster or draw fuller breaths, such as when you are playing hard or when you're afraid. Why do you think you move more air in and out of your lungs at those times?

Perform Bottle Magic and Fool Your Friends

Invite some friends over and trick them with a bit of science magic.

You'll need:

A 1-liter clear plastic soft drink bottle
A pushpin
Kitchen sink

Before your friends come, use the pushpin to poke a hole in the side of the bottle just above the reinforced bottom.

Now you're ready to do the trick for your audience. Ask everyone to stand around the kitchen sink.

Fill the sink nearly full of water. Hold the bottle under the faucet to fill it completely full. Be careful not to squeeze the bottle, because water will squirt out the hole, and you don't want your friends to know about the hole.

Now hold your fingers over the bottle's mouth while you quickly dunk it underwater.

Next, turn the bottle so it's upside down. **Be sure your finger is now pressed over the tiny hole, sealing it.**

Lift the bottle slowly, showing your friends that the water does not run out of the bottle until the mouth is above the surface of the water and air can slip inside.

Plunge the bottle back underwater to show that this stops the water from pouring out.

Now, refill the bottle. Ask for a volunteer from the audience to try to start and stop the water flow just as you did.

Unless your friend happens to put a finger over the hole, the "trick" won't work. As long as air is able to slip in through the hole, water will pour out of the bottle even while its mouth is underwater.

Your friends will be stumped. How did *you* do it?

Of course, when air enters the bottle through the hole, it pushes water out and creates bubbles. If your friends see bubbles, your secret is out.

Magnify It

Is there something tiny you'd like to be able to see better? Science and a bottle can help you.

You'll need:

A 2-liter clear plastic bottle
A piece of newspaper

Fill the bottle nearly full of water and set it on a table or counter. Hold the newspaper close to one side of the bottle. Look at the print through the bottle. The print will appear bigger.

The reason the print appears enlarged is that light rays reflected off the paper are bent as they pass through the curved sides of the bottle and the water. This makes the image seem to be stretched by tricking your eyes into thinking that the light is coming from a bigger area.

A lens or magnifying glass works the same way — the more the lens is curved, the more it appears to stretch the object.

How else has the bottle magnifier changed the way the print looks? Move the printed page closer and farther away; up and down. Does this change the way the print looks? Now look at a picture instead of words. In what ways does the bottle magnifier change the way the picture looks?

Now use your bottle magnifier to look at different objects, such as your finger . . . a penny . . . a strand of your hair and a hair from your cat or dog . . . a feather . . . a stamp. What do you see that you couldn't see before?

Make Your Own Thermos

Need to keep soup hot or a soft drink cold? A thermos can do both. Do you wonder why it's so good at keeping temperatures from changing? Make your own thermos and find out.

You'll need:

A large glass or plastic jar with wide mouth
and lid (such as a pickle container)
A 12-inch square of corrugated cardboard
(from a box)
2 identical cans or bottles of juice, 6 ounces
or less
Scissors
Aluminum foil
An old newspaper

Chill the juice containers for at least an hour.

Cut the cardboard into squares that will fit through the mouth of the jar. Stack these up on the bottom of the jar.

Next, wrap one juice container in three layers of aluminum foil.

Place the wrapped container inside the jar on top of the cardboard. (Remove layers of cardboard as needed so the juice container is below the mouth of the jar.)

Crumple the newspaper and pack it tightly around the juice on all sides.

Tightly seal the lid of the jar. Set the other container of juice next to the sealed jar but without touching it.

After an hour, take the juice out of your homemade thermos. Take off the aluminum foil* and feel the outside of both juice containers. Which feels colder?

*Save the aluminum foil to use again or recycle.

Pour a glass of juice from each container. Taste them. Which tastes colder?

Like a real thermos, the one you made surrounded the juice with materials that are insulators, meaning they don't transfer heat energy easily.

Usually a thermos has double glass walls with a vacuum (a space containing absolutely nothing, not even air) between them. The glass walls are also silvered on the inner surface. Like a mirror, this shiny surface reflects the heat energy. The stopper is made of cork or plastic — materials that slow the transfer of heat.

Make Liquid Art

Pour a tablespoonful of vegetable oil into a glass of water. Did it surprise you to see that the oil floats on the surface of the water? Although many materials will dissolve in water, oil won't. And since it's less dense than water, the oil floats on top.

By adding oil to colored water, you can create a fluid, ever-changing work of art.

You'll need:

A small bottle with a tight cap (can be plastic
    or glass)
Clear vegetable oil
Red, yellow, or green food coloring
A teaspoonful of glitter
Colored beads, small scraps of colored plastic
    (such as bits of cut-up plastic bottles),
    small colorful buttons, or plastic toys

Fill the bottle half full of water and add
enough of one food color to make the water
a vivid hue.

Add enough oil to fill the bottle partway
up the neck.

Dump in the glitter and other items.
Screw the cap on tight.

To set your liquid art in motion, hold the neck in one hand and the base in the other and tip the bottle from side to side. Do this very slowly at first and then a little harder.

What happens to the items you added?

What happens to the water and oil as they move together?

Hold the bottle still and watch the changes that take place as the solution slows down. What else might you put into the bottle to add to this artistic show?

Make a Fountain
in a Bottle

You don't notice the weight of the air pushing on you from all directions — but it does. You can do this demonstration to prove that air exerts pressure.

Fill a glass with water. Get an index card or a piece of cardboard that is slightly larger than the opening and place it over the glass. Hold the card in place with your fingertips while you turn the glass straight upside-down. Then take your fingers away from the card.

Try this outdoors or over a sink because if you don't have the glass straight up and down, it won't work. If you do, the card will keep the water from rushing out. The secret is that the air pressure pushing up on the card exerts more force than the water does pushing down.

Now, use the force that air exerts to create a fountain inside a bottle.

You'll need:

2 clear plastic soft drink bottles (1-liter size)
Modeling clay
2 plastic straws
A pushpin (map tack)
Blue food coloring
Duct tape (optional)

First you need to punch holes in each straw using the pushpin. Start about an inch from the end of the straw. Punch about a dozen holes all the way around the straw. Make the holes in several rows. Wiggle the pin to enlarge the holes.

Next, shape a ball of clay about as big as the neck of the bottles. Press one straw against the side of this ball. Shape the clay so it surrounds the straw, *but be sure the clay does not cover the opening of the straw.* Also, be sure the holes in the straw are below the clay.

Now press the other straw
into the clay ball opposite the
first straw. Make it stick
straight up.

Fill one bottle three-quarters full of water.
Add enough coloring to make the water
bright blue. Put the clay cap onto the bottle
with the straw pointed straight down into
the water.

Turn the other bottle upside down, sliding the neck over the second straw. Push the top bottle into the clay. Press more clay around the bottles to seal the necks. You may want to wrap duct tape over the clay to help secure it.

Working at the kitchen sink, carefully turn the pair of bottles over so the one with water is on top. Watch what happens.

Gravity causes the water in the top bottle to drain into the bottom bottle. When the water level falls below the open end of the straw, though, water begins to spurt out the straw.

This happens because as the amount of water in the bottle goes down, the remaining air expands. The air pushes down on the remaining water. Some is forced into the small holes you made in the straw and up through the straw. When it reaches the top of the straw, it spurts out.

To keep on watching this action, turn the bottles over so the top bottle is the one full of water again.

How to Cut a Bottle in Two

For each of the next three activities you will need to cut apart a 2-liter plastic bottle. You need a ruler, a marker, and a pair of sharp scissors.

Here's what you do:

Measure as the directions tell you to do and make a mark on the side of the bottle. Then draw a line around the bottle at that mark.

Ask an adult to cut the top piece off along the line.

Then you're ready to do the activity.

(1) Poke a hole with the scissors.
(2) Cut along the line.

Make a Bottle Flowerpot

Usually when you water a plant, the water goes down through the soil to the base of the pot. Not with this flowerpot! The water goes from the base up through the soil. How does this happen? Do the activity and see.

You'll need:

A 2-liter soft drink bottle
    (label and cap removed)
A marker
A ruler
Scissors with sharp points
Potting soil
An old cotton tube sock
A small house plant,
    such as an African violet

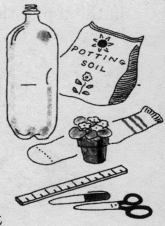

First, you need to cut the bottle apart to make a pot for your plant. Measure about four inches down from the top and make a mark. Measure six inches up from the base and make another mark. (Follow the directions on page 42 for cutting the bottle.)

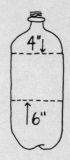

Next, cut a strip of the sock about three inches wide and eight inches long.

Turn the top piece of the bottle upside down. Push the cotton strip through the bottle neck so only about three inches remain in the top of the bottle.

Set this piece in the bottle's base. Spoon in enough potting soil to fill the top piece halfway.

Place your plant in the center and carefully add soil around it, completely covering the roots. Gently pat down the soil so it will help support the plant.

Finally, lift up the top piece and fill the base about half full of water. Push the cotton strip down into the water as you set the plant back onto the base.

To see what will be happening to your plant, fill a glass with water and add enough food coloring to turn it a bright hue. Then touch just the edge of a paper towel to the top of the colored water. As you watch, the water will slowly creep up the paper.

This happens because the water touching the paper moves up into the tiny spaces between the fibers. Because water molecules, the tiny building blocks of water, tend to stick together, more water moves up into the paper. This pushes the first water molecules higher, and slowly this process makes the water climb to the top of the paper towel.

Water moves through the cotton strip into the soil this same way. As the plant's roots take in water, the process continues to pull up water from the base. Just remember to add more water to the base once in a while and your plant will have just the amount of water it needs at all times.

Add a little fertilizer to the water from time to time to keep the plant supplied with the chemicals, such as nitrogen, that it needs to be healthy.

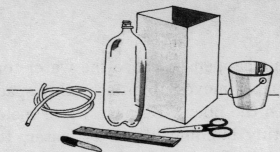

Make an Amazing Water-Producing Box

Do you believe a box can produce water? With the help of science, you can make your friends believe you've made one that does.

You'll need:

A 2-liter plastic bottle
Scissors with sharp points
A cardboard box deep enough to hide the bottle after its top is cut off
A ruler
A marker
2 feet of 1/2-inch flexible plastic tubing (available in stores that sell aquarium or garden supplies)
A plastic bucket
Blue food coloring (optional)

Ask an adult to cut the top off the bottle just below where it flares out. (See cutting directions on page 42.)

Make a hole in the side of the bottle two inches below the top. The hole should be big enough for the tubing to slide through easily.

Place the bottle inside the box. Mark the spot on the box that's directly opposite the hole in the bottle. Cut a matching hole in the box.

Slide the tube through the box and into the bottle inside the box. Make sure the end of the tube doesn't quite touch the bottom of the bottle.

Fill the bottle with water to just below the hole.

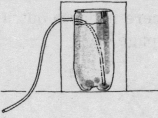

Place the box on a table with a plastic bucket or wastebasket under the end of the tube.

To be sure no one can look inside the box, close the lid or put an oversized piece of stiff cardboard on top.

Now get the top piece of the bottle. This piece will be used as a funnel. Place it with the neck down on the lid of the box and trace around the neck. Cut the circle out and fit the bottle neck into the hole.

You're ready to make magic! Tell your friends that you have a magic box that produces water. To get it started, pour water into the funnel just until water starts to flow out the tube. It won't take much additional water.

Once the water level inside the bottle is above the hole, it creates a siphon that keeps the water flowing.

Just for fun, measure exactly how much water you pour in the funnel. Then have a friend collect the water by cupfuls before dumping it to demonstrate how much *more* came out.

To make your magic water-producing box even more magical, add blue food coloring to the water in the reservoir.

To work, a siphon needs two things:

(1) The section of the tube that's extending down from the hole in the box must be longer than the part inside the bottle that goes up to the hole.

(2) There must be air pressure pushi_ down on the water inside the bottle so there's no break in the column of water flowing through the tube.

As long as these two conditions are met, the siphon will keep the water flowing until the reservoir has been drained.

Raise Sea Monkeys

"Sea monkey" is the nickname sometimes given to tiny brine shrimp. These little shrimp are among the few kinds of animals able to live in Utah's Great Salt Lake, where the water is, on the average, ten percent saltier than the oceans.

These lively critters are also easy to raise at home. Just start up a bottle aquarium and watch the action. Then try the experiment to learn even more about brine shrimp.

You'll need:

A 2-liter clear plastic bottle
A ruler
A marker
Scissors with sharp points
A spoon
Measuring spoons
Two tablespoons rock salt, or kosher salt
Brine shrimp eggs (inexpensive and available at pet shops that sell aquarium supplies because they're raised to feed tropical fish)
A magnifying glass
A package of dry yeast

Cut the top off the bottle about two inches below the neck. (See the directions on page 42.) Be sure the bottle is clean.

Fill the bottle nearly full of water and let it sit for a day. Add the rock salt and stir until it's completely dissolved. Sprinkle 1/4 teaspoon of brine shrimp eggs on the surface of the water. Place the bottle in a warm spot that isn't directly in the sun.

Over the next few days, watch for signs of movement in the bottle. The newly hatched shrimp will be very tiny, but you'll be able to see them swimming in a jerky up-and-down motion.

Feed the shrimp by sprinkling a few grains of powdered yeast on the water every third day.

Keep a journal of your observations. How many days did it take for the first eggs to hatch?

As the brine shrimp grow bigger, use your magnifying glass to look for eggs inside the females.

In what other ways do the females look different from the males? How long is it before you see new baby brine shrimp in the water?

You may want to do some more experiments to see what conditions affect how quickly brine shrimp eggs hatch.

Set up three bottles full of brine water just as you did before. Label these 1, 2, and 3.

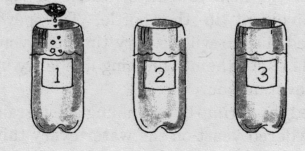

Add an extra tablespoonful of rock salt to bottle 1.

Set bottle 2 in a place that will stay cool.

Put bottle 3 in the dark. Check regularly for newly hatched brine shrimp. Did any hatch more quickly than in your original batch? Which was the slowest to hatch? Of course, you'll need to repeat this test two more times to be sure that the results you got are likely to happen every time.

Now, plan a test using ice and one using a flashlight to test how temperature and exposure to bright light affect brine shrimp behavior. Don't forget to repeat these tests, too. Record the results in your journal.

Fast Facts About Brine Shrimp

- Brine shrimp live throughout the world, wherever there is very salty water. In the Great Salt Lake, there are sometimes so many brine shrimp that they make the water appear red or brownish-red. This color is created by the green algae the brine shrimp eat. During the digestion process the algae turns red. Since the brine shrimp are nearly transparent, this color shows.

- Brine shrimp eggs are very hardy. They can withstand being baked by the sun or exposed to freezing winter temperatures and still hatch.

- The curator of the Steinhart Aquarium of the California Academy of Sciences was the first to discover that brine shrimp make good food for aquarium fishes. Besides being cheap and easy to raise, brine shrimp don't decay and pollute the tank if they aren't eaten immediately. Since the tiny shrimp are alive, they just keep on swimming around, providing in-between-meal snacks for hungry fish.